CHEVROLE STATION WAGONS
1946 THROUGH 1966
PHOTO ARCHIVE

by Robert J. Headrick, Jr.

Iconografix

Photo Archive Series

Iconografix
PO Box 446
Hudson, Wisconsin 54016 USA

Library of Congress Card Number: 2001135738

ISBN 1-58388-069-0

02 03 04 05 06 07 08 5 4 3 2 1

Printed in China

Cover and book design by Shawn Glidden

Copyediting by Suzie Helberg

COVER PHOTO: 1948 Chevrolet Fleetmaster station wagon, model #2109.

BOOK PROPOSALS

Iconografix is a publishing company specializing in books for transportation enthusiasts. We publish in a number of different areas, including Automobiles, Auto Racing, Buses, Construction Equipment, Emergency Equipment, Farming Equipment, Railroads & Trucks. The Iconografix imprint is constantly growing and expanding into new subject areas.

Authors, editors, and knowledgeable enthusiasts in the field of transportation history are invited to contact the Editorial Department at Iconografix, Inc., PO Box 446, Hudson, WI 54016.

DEDICATION

To Frank—thanks for letting me park the '54 Bel Air Townsman station wagon in your space in the garage, good weather and bad. And to my parents—thanks for all of our station wagon memories!

ACKNOWLEDGMENTS

No book is ever written without help, and this certainly is the case with this one. A special thanks goes to Ken Luttermoser, General Motors Media Archives. His quick responses to my requests enabled me to secure the necessary photos from the General Motors Media Archives to illustrate this history of Chevrolet station wagons.

Special thanks also goes to Mark Patrick, Curator, National Automotive History Collection, Detroit Public Library, who made many files accessible to me during my visit to the collection and to Mark Benner, Campbell-Ewald Advertising, for helping to secure permission from Chevrolet Motor Division to use sales and advertising materials.

I also want to thank Chris at Ken McGee's Holdings and Sharon at McLellan's Automotive History for always being able to find just the right materials I requested and then getting them to me as quickly as possible.

Finally, a book like this includes a great deal of facts, and in order to determine the accuracy of those facts,

I referred frequently to the following excellent resources, some of which are now out of print:

A Pictorial History of Chevrolet 1940-1954, John D. Robertson (1998)
Bowties of the Fifties, James H. Moloney (2000)
Chevrolet Book of Numbers, Volume 2, David Cummings, Jr., (1989)
Chevrolet Chronicle: A Pictorial History From 1904, Arch Brown, Pat Chappell, Bob Hall (1991)
Chevrolet: USA-1, Ray Miller (1982)
Chevrolet 1950-1959, Byron Olsen (1996)
Illustrated Chevrolet Buyer's Guide, John Gunnell (1989)
Standard Catalog of Chevrolet 1912-1998, Edited by Ron Kowalke (1998)
Station Wagon: A Tribute to America's Workaholic on Wheels, Ron Kowalke (1998)
The Station Wagon: Its Saga and Development, Bruce Briggs (1975)
Station Wagons, Byron Olsen and Dan Lyons (2000)

Robert J. Headrick, Jr.
St. Louis, Missouri
October 2001

INTRODUCTION

Perhaps you've wondered what a "station wagon" really is? Bruce Briggs in *The Station Wagon: Its Saga and Development*, offers the following definition: "The generally accepted concept of a station wagon is a passenger-carrying vehicle, which also converts to a cargo carrier. We think of a tailgate for rear loading and seats that are removable or convert to provide more luggage space." Ron Kowalke adds to this definition by providing the following characteristics for both the vehicle and the seats—"the American station wagon—in its truest form—is defined as a long-wheelbase, rear-driven vehicle, most often having third-seat availability. That third seat is either forward- or rear-facing, or, in some instances, dual-center facing." Based on these definitions each of the Chevrolet station wagons discussed and illustrated in this book qualifies for inclusion. The purpose for each wagon is to carry both people and cargo. Early examples of station wagons appeared more truck- or bus-like. This was certainly the case early in the history of the American station wagon. However, Byron Olsen, in *Station Wagons*, is quick to point out that "the story of the American station wagon tracks the evolution of the American automobile. From a utilitarian truck-like vehicle, to a car-based vehicle, to a style statement, and finally to a universal family vehicle is the story line of the American station wagon." Telling this story line through pictures is the intent of this book.

The illustrations selected in many cases offer more than just a picture of a particular Chevrolet station wagon. The background, the setting, the people, and the actions of the people all combine to create an image of the car and how that image might become a part of our lives. We were encouraged to fantasize about what it would be like to drive this car or to park it in our driveway. What would the neighbors think when they saw the car in our driveway? What would it say about us socially? Economically? According to Heon Stevenson, in *Selling the Dream: Advertising the American Automobile 1930-1980*, Chevrolet's general advertising philosophy for the 1950s was "to provide the most car for the least money." And, in the illustrations used to sell Chevrolet from 1950-1959 there was "a continued emphasis on fun, sociability and a

modern, though not exclusive, lifestyle." Indeed the illustrations used to tell the story of Chevrolet also told our story.

As you look at the illustrations for a particular year, notice how the details in the illustration help to establish the role the wagon was playing at a point in time. Nineteen fifties wagons are placed in realistic settings—at the beach, in cities, at historic monuments, or at the park. The actions, too, are realistic—shopping, hauling lots of cargo, car-pooling, and vacations. Mid-1950s advertising placed more emphasis on suburban activities with increased attention paid to highlighting the necessity of a station wagon to carry out the tasks associated with suburban living. "By 1958, the station wagon was firmly entrenched as an integral part of America's expanding suburban landscape and, to remain socially acceptable, it had to become fashion-conscious," according to Stevenson. In much of this marketing copy, evident in both ads and dealership sales brochures, there was an implication "that the man who provided for his family ought not to deny his wife and children the independence and convenience that ownership of a wagon provided." (229, Stevenson)

The shift from the utilitarian purpose of a station wagon to one of suburban chic, as Stevenson referred to it, occurred in the 1960s with an emphasis on comfort, accessories, engines, and transmissions—with illustrations often placing the station wagon in an environmental setting. There seems to have become, according to Stevenson, "a standard layout... a photograph of the car against a realistic—if socially optimized-background, a slogan, and a few paragraphs of copy at the foot of the page. Technical and status differentiation was increasingly established within the copy itself..."

Take time now to journey through the story of the *Chevrolet Station Wagon, 1946-1966*. Perhaps as you do so there will be times when you too will once again recall a trip you and your family made in a Chevrolet Station Wagon.

The 1946 Fleetmaster station wagon, of which there were 804 produced, cost $1,712, making it the most expensive model. Chevrolet actually began station wagon production on a passenger car chassis in 1939, but this model, available on either the Master Deluxe or Master 86 chassis, appeared only in the truck catalog. The first postwar Chevrolet was built on October 3, 1945.

In 1946, Chevrolet offered buyers "big car quality at the lowest price." Mechanically, the 1946 models were virtually the same as in 1942, except that a different carburetor was used. The series names were changed. Master Deluxe became Stylemaster, Special Deluxe became Fleetmaster, and Fleetline became the top-of-the-line.

Instrument panel layout of the 1946 Fleetmaster station wagon was exactly like that of the 1942 wagon. There is an ashtray centered between the speedometer (left) and clock (right). Note this is a radio-delete model. A Di-noc imitation woodgrain was used on the top of the dash and the doorsills.

Ad copy for 1947 extolled the virtues of the new 1947 Chevrolet station wagon—"...big-car quality at lowest cost." The 1947 Chevrolet station wagon was the only station wagon with a body by Fisher. Prior to 1946, subcontractors produced the wooden bodies of Chevrolet's station wagons.

The 1947 Chevrolet station wagon (model #2109) can quickly be distinguished from the 1946 model by a redesigned hood ornament, a cleaner reconfigured grille, and the absence of the side trim strips. Production increased to 4,912 units on Chevrolet's most expensive, and at the same time, least popular model. Before station wagons became the "preferred mode of transportation" for the American family, there were many utilitarian uses—here a group of hunters prepares for the hunt.

Like its predecessors, this 1947 Chevrolet Fleetmaster station wagon's body consisted of ash and mahogany panels with a weatherproof leatherette top stretched over wooden slats. Imitation woodgraining—on inside door frames—and imitation leather seats made for a very attractive interior. Like all wood-bodied cars the upkeep required considerable effort on the part of the owner. Remarkably, many wagons did survive the abuse that was all too frequent, and today these models are highly prized and expensive collectibles. Note the three seats—the second and third seats are removable.

This couple was probably the envy of the neighborhood back in 1947. Dealers introduced the new models on February 8, 1947.

Advertising suggested in 1948 that "Chevrolet, and only Chevrolet, is First!," and although actual production was up almost 12 percent, the total was still less than the 1935 figure. The 1948 model line-up remained the same with only a minor change in the grille with the addition of a vertical "T-bar" added. This 1948 Chevrolet Fleetmaster model, an attractive one to say the least, features several options including a grille guard, fog lights, rear-view mirror (driver-side), white wall tires, chrome wheel rings, and chrome gravel guards. There were 10,171 1948 station wagons produced; more than doubling the previous year's number. Each wagon sold for $2,013.

By the late 1930s the concept of a station wagon was changing. Its commercial role, which was largely that of hauling people, began to fade and the station wagons of the 1940s and thereafter became more stylish and associated with pleasure travel. More wood-bodied wagons might have been sold if they had been cheaper and required less maintenance. In most cases the wood on these wagons had to be re-varnished yearly, and if this wasn't enough, the wood-bodied wagon was quick to rattle and squeak. New Fleetmaster station wagon models for 1948 were introduced in February 1948. Engineering Enterprises of Detroit, Michigan offered a woodgrain "Country Club" kit for those drivers who wanted the "Woody" look on their convertible or sedan. The kit, a dealer-installed accessory, cost $149.50. There were few takers, but this did, nevertheless, attest to the popularity of the woodgrained station wagons.

There were many changes for Chevrolet in 1949. There were 14 models now in two series and all model names were changed. The new Styleline series included notchback sedans, coupes, station wagons, and a convertible. The Fleetline series no longer applied to the top-of-the-line, but now referred to the fastback models. Both new series were available in "special" or "deluxe" trim versions. A nameplate on the front fenders could identify the new "deluxe" series. Early 1949 Chevrolet literature offered the station wagon in two different versions: the all-wood body (model #2109) and the new steel-body version (model #2119). The Ionia models, #2109, were built until mid-year and then replaced with the steel-body version, #2119, that featured simulated woodgrain trim. Compare the two versions by looking at the photographs on pages 14 and 15. In order to distinguish the two, examine the shape of the dark-paneled indentations on the wood-body car (page 14) to those on the steel-body version (page 15).

The new steel-bodied 1949 Styleline Deluxe station wagon featured mahogany door and quarter trim panels, leather fabric headliner, simulated woodgrain roof bows, and brown simulated leather seats. The spare tire was located in a recessed panel under the rear floor. The two rear-most seats could be removed to accommodate larger cargo.

THE STATION WAGON

Only its quietness, durability and ease of maintenance tell you that this eight-passenger Station Wagon body is all-steel. For it is painted and grained as shown to look exactly like wood. Four doors, of course, and removable rear seats for extra hauling space when you want it.

There was little to distinguish the 1950 Chevrolet Styleline Deluxe station wagon from its predecessor (a new grille, hood and trunk ornaments, and minor trim changes). Yet production and sales numbers set records with nearly 1.5 million cars produced. In 1950, Chevrolet introduced its now famous Powerglide automatic transmission, available for the first time in the low-price field, but available only on the DeLuxe models. The 1950 station wagon, model #2119, was very similar to the 1949 steel-bodied model. Actual production numbers for 1950 are estimated to be around 35,000 units and the selling price $1,994.

About the only distinguishable changes from 1950 to 1951 were the movement of the parking lights to the outer edges of the lower grille molding and a non-glare instrument panel. Most Fleetline models were discontinued mid-year because of sluggish sales. The 1951 station wagon remained the most expensive model at $2,191 but saw decreased sales at 23,586 units. This restored wagon features an outside visor trimmed in stainless steel. New, the visor cost a whopping $19.95: today such a feature often sells for more than $500. The "Impala" hood ornament appeared in 1951; the owner could, however, order a special "Gazelle" for an additional $7.80. The simulated woodgrain took on a darker hue in 1951.

The seats in a 1951 Styleline Deluxe station wagon were done in imitation leather with tan rubber floor mats. The headliner consisted of simulated leather with roof bows finished in a woodgrain pattern. This same woodgrain pattern was repeated on the door garnish moldings. Seating allowed for eight, with the second and third seats removable, thus allowing for increased cargo space.

Chevrolet proposed this modification of a 1951 Styleline Deluxe station wagon in order to attract business in the New York City market.

The addition of a few new trim pieces, five teeth added to the central horizontal bar of the grille, a modification of the parking lights, changes in the hood and trunk emblems, "DeLuxe" nameplate appearing on the front quarter panel of DeLuxe models, and several new pastel colors highlight the changes made to the 1952 Chevrolets. Once again, the 1952 Chevrolet Styleline Deluxe station wagon, model #2119, saw decreased production (almost by half), with a total of 12,756 units released at a price of $2,297. Materials were short in 1952 because of the Korean Conflict, most notably in the absence of white wall tires and the elimination of nickel in the plating process of chrome, which caused many chrome pieces to turn black in a short period of time. The station wagon was available in four colors: Emerald Green, Sahara Beige, Saddle Brown, and Regal Maroon.

A cutaway shot of the interior of a 1952 Styleline Deluxe Chevrolet station wagon. This layout is typical of the wagons of this period. Both the second (intermediate) and third (rear) seats are removable, thus allowing for increased space for hauling cargo. The seats are covered in imitation brown leather with rubber mats on the floors and actual wood panels on the doors. The door garnish moldings are made of steel with a woodgrain paint finish.

Chevrolet *presents*

the last words in
station wagons

"Handyman"
(two of them) and

"Townsman"

with wonderful new
features you'll want

THE "TWO-TEN" HANDYMAN . . .

One of three great new all-steel station wagons . . . *all* offering new high-compression power . . . four-door convenience . . . and such features as Power Steering.* (6 passengers—*folding rear seat.*)

THE TOWNSMAN . . .

Plenty of room for eight. Advanced 108-h.p. "Thrift-King" engine with standard gearshift, or new 115-h.p. "Blue-Flame" engine with Powerglide automatic transmission.* (*Simulated wood-grain trim—removable center and rear seat.*)

CHEVROLET

MORE PEOPLE BUY CHEVROLETS
THAN ANY OTHER CAR!

THE "ONE-FIFTY" HANDYMAN . . .

The new, low-priced station wagon in the low-price field . . . and like all other 1953 Chevrolets, offers great new operating economy. (6 passengers—*folding rear seat.*)

Chevrolet Division of General Motors, Detroit 2, Michigan

*Optional at extra cost. Combination of Powerglide automatic transmission and 115-h.p. "Blue-Flame" engine available on "Two-Ten" and Bel Air models. Power Steering available on all models. Combination of standard equipment and trim illustrated is dependent on availability of material.

HOLIDAY/AUGUST

In 1953 there were three wagons from which to select. The entry-level wagon, the One-Fifty series Handyman and the mid-level wagons, the Two-Ten series Handyman and the Townsman. The basic engine for 1953 was the Blue Flame Six with 108-horsepower in the standard transmission and 115-horsepower in the Powerglide models. Although each wagon used the same 4-door shell, there were significant trim differences in each model. Dealer introductions of the new wagons began in January 1953.

THE TOWNSMAN . . .

The top-of-the-line model of the 1953 station wagons was the Two-Ten Townsman. This was an 8-passenger model, with removable intermediate and rear seats. This was the only model to have simulated woodgrain exterior trim and painted woodgrain interior roof bows and door garnish moldings, otherwise it bore the same trim as the Two-Ten series and was generally identified as a Two-Ten. The most expensive model in the Chevrolet line-up for 1953 at $2,273; there were 7,988 produced.

The intermediate-level station wagon, the 1953 Two-Ten Handyman, was described as having "deluxe appointments" and practical utility. This wagon featured a folding rear seat and was a 6-passenger model. 18,258 units were produced at a cost of $2,123 each. Buyers of the Two-Ten Handyman and Townsman wagons could also order power steering, another option offered by Chevrolet to the low-priced field, at a cost of $178… this price probably accounted for its limited popularity.

The folding rear seat, first offered by Chevrolet in 1953, offered increased cargo hauling space. Note also that the spare tire was now housed under the rear cargo area. Lifting up the cover exposed a recess in which the spare tire was stored.

The 1953 Two-Ten Handyman station wagon continued to demonstrate its usefulness in a variety of ways. Note how the addition of white wall tires adds to the attractiveness of this wagon.

The lowest-priced wagon in 1953, also a 6-passenger car with folding rear seat, was the One-Fifty Handyman. Typical of entry-level vehicles, the One-Fifty series was devoid of bright trim around the windows and on the body. This wagon was the most popular with a total of 22,408 produced at a cost of $2,010 a piece. The One-Fifty Handyman station wagon had safety sheet side windows.

This modified version of a 1953 Chevrolet station wagon with its side spears was created for Dinah Shore, who sang the popular Chevrolet slogan song, "See the USA in Your Chevrolet." This slogan first appeared in print ads in 1951. This modified version was actually put into production as the 1954 Bel Air Townsman station wagon.

THE BEL AIR TOWNSMAN

In 1954, Chevrolet celebrated the production of its 30-millionth car. Minor exterior changes included: new hubcaps, reflective strip on taillights, new grille with wraparound parking light housings, new bumpers and bumper guards, new hood and trunk emblems, and a new hood ornament. The 2-door utility sedan replaced the Business Coupe, and there was a horsepower increase to both engines (108 to 115) on the standard version and (115 to 125) on the Powerglide version. Power brakes ($38), power windows, front windows only ($86), power front seat ($86), and a reduced cost for power steering (from $178 to $135) were offered to Chevrolet buyers in 1954. There were still three wagons from which to select: the One-Fifty series Handyman, the Two-Ten series Handyman, and the new Bel Air Townsman, formerly a Two-Ten series model, but now offered in the Bel Air line.

THE "ONE-FIFTY" HANDYMAN

The 1954 One-Fifty Handyman, model #1509, cost $2,020 and attracted 21,404 buyers. Two-tone paint schemes were popular... here the wagon is light over dark.

Another version of the 1954 One-Fifty series Handyman station wagon: this time with a dark top over light body. Note again how white wall tires dress this car up.

The 1954 Two-Ten Handyman station wagon, model # 2109, cost $2,133 and was the most popular wagon in 1954. A total of 27,175 Two-Ten wagons were produced. With the rear seat folded and the tailgate down there is space for cargo eight feet in length. Interiors were upholstered in longwearing vinyl of contrasting colors and textures.

30

By the mid-1950s, station wagons were becoming an integral part of the expanding suburban landscape.

The 1954 Townsman was no longer a Two-Ten series wagon. In 1954 it became the most expensive vehicle in the Chevrolet line, excluding of course the Corvette. Now a Bel Air series wagon, the Townsman, #2419, cost $2,283. An 8-passenger car with three seats (the intermediate and rear were removable), the Townsman station wagon was the last Chevrolet wagon to bear woodgrain trim. However, woodgrain trim would reappear in 1966 on the Caprice station wagon.

A nice view of the simulated woodgrain trim on the 1954 Bel Air Townsman station wagon. The car, however, is not as striking without whitewall tires. This was the first year that an automatic transmission was available in all Chevrolet models. It was also the last year for the exclusive use of the 6-cylinder engine in Chevrolet.

Again, the versatility of the station wagon is demonstrated by its surroundings. Whether at a roadside vegetable stand or at the country club, the 1954 Chevrolet Bel Air Townsman was at home. Note what a difference the presence of white wall tires makes.

The 1954 Bel Air Townsman was available in three solid colors (Bermuda Green, Shoreline Beige and Saddle Brown) and three two-tone colors (Shoreline Beige over Bermuda Green, India Ivory over Horizon Blue, and Shoreline Beige over Saddle Brown).

THE NEW BEL AIR TOWNSMAN,
a stylish new star in the station wagon field

Just the ticket for those trips to the wide open spaces

Going places is more fun than ever—when you go in Chevrolet's new Bel Air Townsman.

This roomy 4-door carries 8 passengers comfortably. Or minus the easily removed rear seats, it hauls up to half a ton of cargo. The Townsman is rugged and husky, packed with Chevrolet's high-compression power—the *highest* compression power in any leading low-priced car. As you know, higher compression means more power and more miles out of every gallon of gas. Performance is finer, economy greater!

And it's every inch a Chevrolet Bel Air with its distinctive styling, and its handsome, color-matched interiors of long-wearing vinyl. No doubt about it, the Townsman is designed to add more pleasure, more comfort and more convenience to every mile you drive. Why not look it over soon at your Chevrolet dealer's. . . . Chevrolet Division of General Motors, Detroit 2, Michigan.

YEAR AFTER YEAR MORE PEOPLE BUY CHEVROLETS THAN ANY OTHER CAR!

CHEVROLET

THE THRILLING CHEVROLET CORVETTE—FIRST ALL-AMERICAN SPORTS CAR
It's America's Number One Fun Car

A rare advertisement for the 1954 Chevrolet Bel Air Townsman. The ad copy extols the virtues of owning a Townsman... it adds "more pleasure, more comfort and more convenience to every mile you drive."

The year 1955 was a big year for Chevrolet and General Motors. Under the leadership of Ed Cole the engineering team, which grew from 850 to almost 3,000 engineers, designed Chevrolet's new V-8 engine, drive train, and chassis in just under 15 weeks. Totally new styling debuted on the full-size cars and there were now five "Stylish Wagons by Chevrolet" to select from.

The 1955 Nomad, a 2-door Bel Air wagon, advertised as "A Beautiful Addition to Any Resort," arrived in mid-1955 and was, according to *Motor Trend* magazine, "the longed-for styling wedding between the production sports car and the family workhorse." Available only in a 2-door version, 8,386 units were produced, making it the second lowest production car in 1955.

Just Look at what CHEVROLET has done to the Station Wagon

The 1955 Nomad, modeled after a concept car that was making its way on the auto show circuit, offered many unique features including: lots of glass area, cut-out rear wheel openings, convertible-style windows, bright metal eyebrows over the headlights, and seven stainless moldings on the tailgate.

The 1955 Nomad was the most expensive model for the year, delivering for $2,571. The trend-setter of the 1955 wagons, Chevrolet described the new Nomad as the "peak of style and grace, its swept-forward windows, grooved top, and softly sloping back lend true sportsman's flair... its rich fabric interiors and dazzling colors make it the fashion achievement of station wagon styling." Load length is increased by almost 11 inches when the seats are folded flush with the floor.

Look again at how wide the tailgate opens and also at the amount of cargo space. Plenty of room—an all-purpose family car the year 'round.

The Bel Air wagon for 1955 was called the Beauville, model #2409. At a cost of $2,262 there were 24,313 Bel Air wagons produced, almost three times as many as in 1954. For the first time, the second seat in the wagons folded flush with the floor. Other features new for 1955 included 12-volt electrical system, high-level ventilation system, tubeless tires, knee-action front suspension, and air conditioning. The year 1955 was the year of two-tone paint schemes. Not fully anticipated by Chevrolet, the early release sales catalogs featured only a few two tone versions, and this was the traditional pattern of the roof painted a different color from the body. By mid-year, however, two-tone paint jobs were the rage with India Ivory in combination with red, yellow, black and turquoise. Other popular two-tone schemes included Shadow Gray and Coral, Skyline Blue and Glazier Blue, and Neptune Green and Sea-mist Green. Popular wagon combinations included Shoreline Beige and Autumn Bronze, Shoreline Beige and Gypsy Red, and Glazier Blue and Skyline Blue.

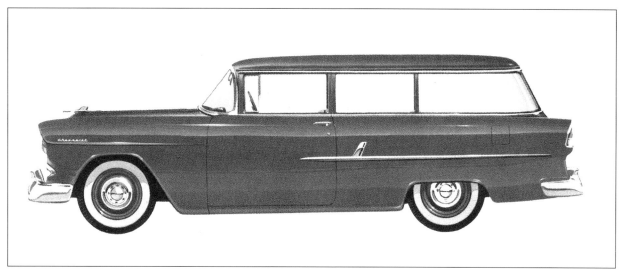

There were two versions of the 1955 Two-Ten station wagon, the 2-door Handyman and the 4-door Townsman (models #2129 and #2109 respectively). The 4-door Townsman was the best selling wagon in 1955 with 82,303 units; the 2-door model was second best with 28,918 units.

The 1955 One-Fifty Handyman, model #1529, cost $2,030 and saw 17,936 produced. Bright metal work was limited to Chevrolet script on front fender, chrome-plated bumpers, grille, hood ornament, lamp rims, and wheel hub centers. In 1955 you could select from six different power-drive combinations—the biggest choice in Chevrolet history, and each combination was available on all wagons.

The Hottest Half Dozen in Station Wagons

BEL AIR BEAUVILLE
4 doors, 9 passengers.

Seats a whole baseball team ... *beautifully!*

Chevrolet station wagons really shine, whether carrying a full baseball team (as two different models will), or a half ton of cargo (*all* models can). Your range of choice includes six handsome models (2 doors or 4) from the budget-wise "One-Fifty" Handyman through the glamorous Nomad. All offer you lively V8 or 6 engines (up to 205 h.p.), a choice of fully automatic Powerglide,* Touch-Down Overdrive* or smooth-shifting Synchro-Mesh transmissions. And for greater driving convenience, you have a full selection of the most popular power options. As for colors? There are dozens of attractive solid colors and two-tone combinations. Nowhere else will you find so much in a station wagon as in any one of the "hottest half dozen!" *An extra-cost option.

Advertisements for both Chevrolet and Ford throughout the 1950s and 1960s stressed two areas of modern suburban living—recreation and shopping. Another wagon was added to the line-up in 1956; now there were six wagons to choose from. Styling changes for 1956 included full width grille, rectangular parking lamps, new front and rear bumpers and guards (except the wagons), dome-shaped taillight lenses in chrome housings, and different side trim determined by the model series. Another new feature was the fuel filler door hidden under the left taillight.

Another view of the 1956 Chevrolet Bel Air Beauville. The V-shaped emblem below the hood and deck ornaments indicates the presence of a V-8.

A 1956 Bel Air wagon put into livery for a Chevrolet dealership in Saginaw, Michigan. A trip to any dealership in the 1950s guaranteed that there would be displays of the popular dealer-installed options to dress up your new Chevrolet. Popular options in 1956 included: fender and grille guards, exhaust extension, door edge guards, gasoline door guard, vent shades, body mount mirrors and lights—under the hood, in the trunk, and under the dash when the doors opened.

Shown is an example of a 1956 Chevrolet Bel Air Beauville Station Wagon Interior. Station wagon interiors consisted of vinyl and nylon-faced pattern cloth. Note also the different configurations of seating in the wagons. There was plenty of room for passengers and cargo.

Ready to GO with any cargo!

Three passengers and lots of room to spare.

Six passengers with all their luggage.

Nine passengers (two models carry this many)!

Model #2109, a 4-door 1956 Two-Ten Townsman; a 6-passenger model that cost $2,362. This was the most popular wagon Chevrolet built in 1956 with total production reaching 113,656 units. More than 80 percent of those who purchased a Chevrolet in 1956 preferred the two-tone paint scheme. There were 12 single-tone and 16 two-tone paint choices for 1956. Popular wagon colors included: Onyx Black/Crocus Yellow, Imperial Ivory/Inca Silver, India Ivory/Matador Red, India Ivory/Dusk Plum, Sherwood Green/Pinecrest Green, and Calypso Cream/Grecian Gold. There was a preference for primary colors in 1955, and although other manufacturers went to more pastel colors in 1956, Chevrolet stuck with brighter primary colors.

The 1956 Two-Ten station wagon was also available as a 2-door Handyman, model #2129. A total of 22,038 were produced at a cost of $2,215 each. Like the Bel Air models the floors were covered with vinyl-coated rubber floor mats. All wagons had vinyl upholstery.

The least expensive and least produced wagon in the 1956 line-up was the One-Fifty series 2-door Handyman. For only a few more dollars this same model could be ordered in the Two-Ten series. At a cost of $2,171, there were 13,487 units produced. The most noticeable difference between the Two-Ten and One Fifty series was the absence of the stainless trim on the rear quarter panels.

Again in 1956, the Nomad topped the line-up of station wagons. A total of 7,886 were produced, down 500 from the previous year. Priced at $2,608, concessions were made in 1956 in order to cut production costs of this wagon. These cost-cutting measures included: the chrome eyebrow trim was deleted, the interior was the same as other Bel Air wagons, and the rear wheel sheet metal cut-out was standardized with other models in the 1956 line. Directional signals became regular equipment rather than an option, and a waterproof voltage regulator and electric temperature gauge were added as standard equipment.

Bel Air Nomad

Vertical chromium strips were found only on the Nomad tailgate. The chromium strips were a distinguishing characteristic of the Nomad through 1958. The Nomad wagon body was not shared with any other Chevrolet model until 1958.

Additional views of the 1956 Chevrolet No-mad. From any angle this is an attractive car and today remains very collectible.

After banner years in 1955 (Chevrolet out-sold all the competition) and 1956, the decision to face-lift the 1955 models once again (a modest face-lift produced the 1956 models) in order to use them as 1957 models, threw the Chevrolet design studio into a frenzy. Prior to this, engineers in the studio had been working on an entirely new body design for 1957. A decision was actually made in 1955 based on Chevrolet's not knowing how popular the 1955 models would become, to compete with what GM assumed would be new models from Ford and Plymouth. In actuality, the 1957 design became the 1958 cars, and the 1957 Chevrolets were different in almost every styling detail being mounted on the 1955 body and chassis. There were six station wagon models again in 1957... all with new styling!

For the third and final year, the Nomad appeared as a unique body style. And for the third year running its production decreased, this year to 6,103 units. However, it remained the most expensive model ($2,757) in 1957, almost $250 more than the convertible.

New exterior features for 1957 included a combination bumper and radiator grille integrated with the body, flatter and lower hood with distinctive twin, chrome-ornamented windsplits, chrome body side moldings, and on the Nomad and Bel Air models gold-anodized aluminum ornaments on the front fenders, and fluted aluminum rear-quarter trim panels. The Nomad remained a 2-door wagon making it difficult for passengers to get in or out of the back seat of the car. This is apparently one of the reasons that the Nomad's popularity decreased.

Advertising proclaimed that "For work or play—on any occasion—Chevrolet's got the handiest, dandiest wagons of all!" This family would probably agree! Chevrolet's new automatic transmission, the Turboglide, offered the smoothest performance in the low-price field. There was a variable torque ratio from standstill to cruising offering not the slightest hint of a shift. In 1957, you could also select from the famous Powerglide, overdrive, or conventional 3-speed synchromesh transmissions.

The 1957 Bel Air Townsman (model #2409) was a 4-door, 6-passenger vehicle. A popular wagon with production reaching 27,375, the Townsman sold for $2,580 and was the second highest produced wagon by Chevrolet in 1957. Chevrolet introduced the fuel injection system in 1957, designed to eliminate the need for the carburetor. Unfortunately, this system, like the Turboglide transmission, saw early problems and it took a while to work the bugs out.

Popular two-tone color combinations for 1957 included Harbor Blue/Larkspur Blue, Surf Green/Highland Green, India Ivory/Canyon Coral, Adobe Beige/Sierra Gold, India Ivory/Matador Red, and Colonial Cream/Laurel Green.

From any angle the 1957
Bel Air Townsman station
wagon is an attractive car.

The only 9-passenger wagon for 1957, the Two-Ten Beauville, model #2119. A total of 21,083 were produced at a cost of $2,563 each. Although more stylistically akin to the lower-priced One-Fifty series, the Two-Ten series appeared more like the Bel Air when done up in a two-tone finish.

Picnics were popular in the 1950s. This 1957 Bel Air provides its family with plenty of room for all their picnic necessities.

The 1957 Two-Ten Townsman station wagon (model #2109), a 4-door, 6-passenger car, saw production of 127,803 at a cost of $2,356 each. It was the most popular wagon produced in 1957. From the exterior there was no difference between the Townsman and the Beauville.

The 2-door model in the 1957 Two-Ten series bore the designation "Handyman" (model #2129). Like other wagons it too offered a folding rear seat, thus providing increased space for cargo. At a cost of $2,502, 17,528 were delivered to customers.

Chevrolet offered vehicles for police, taxi, and fleet service. Here is a wagon used by the Army. No options here, even the paint is a single tone, including the inside of the fluted rear-quarter trim panel. Generally these cars came with a 6-cylinder engine and standard transmission for economical reasons. However, in 1957 buyers could select different engines including the 140-horsepower six, a 162-horsepower 265 V-8 (with manual transmission only), and six different versions of the 283 V-8 with 185- to 283-horsepower.

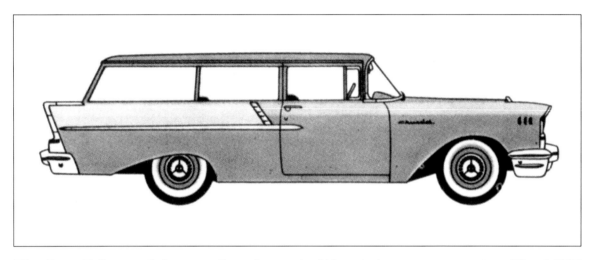

The One-Fifty models were the plainest of the station wagon series. The 1957 One-Fifty Handyman, model #1529, was a 2-door version and cost $2,307; 14,740 were produced.

The body of a 1957 Chevrolet One-Fifty Handyman station wagon on the assembly line.

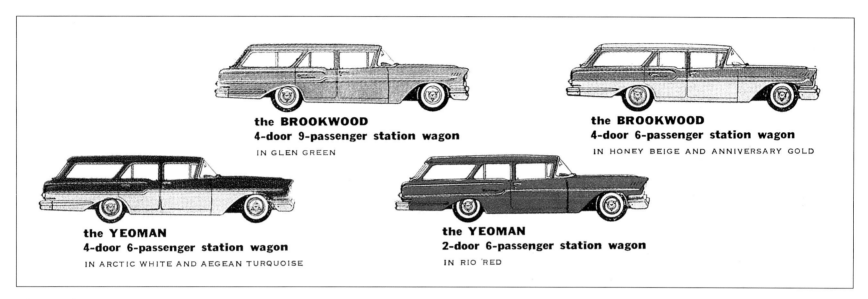

the BROOKWOOD
4-door 9-passenger station wagon

IN GLEN GREEN

the BROOKWOOD
4-door 6-passenger station wagon

IN HONEY BEIGE AND ANNIVERSARY GOLD

the YEOMAN
4-door 6-passenger station wagon

IN ARCTIC WHITE AND AEGEAN TURQUOISE

the YEOMAN
2-door 6-passenger station wagon

IN RIO 'RED

The 1958 Chevrolet station wagons were completely new from the ground up. Chevrolet's competitors were gaining strength and GM made the decision to go forth with a major body redesign. The year 1958 was also when the "big block" 348 cubic-inch V-8 was introduced. Quad headlights made their debut. A new safety-girder frame offered increased stability, and full coil suspension took the bumps out of the ride. But if you really wanted a smoother ride you could select the new Level Air—Chevy's new air suspension system that supposedly put a cushion of air between you and the road. However, if the system failed you couldn't drive the car! Most buyers opted not to purchase the system, which only cost $123.75. Again this year there were five station wagons from which to select—the Nomad, the Brookwood, 6- and 9- passenger models, and the Yeoman, also 6- and 9-passenger models. Now the Nomad's body was identical to the other 1958 Chevrolet wagons. The only 2-door version remaining in the line-up was the Yeoman 6-passenger wagon.

In 1958, the Nomad officially became the Bel Air Nomad. Now a 4-door, 6-passenger model, the Nomad script and tailgate strips were the only vestiges of the 1955-1957 Nomads. New features included gull-wing fenders, new length (almost ten inches longer than the 1957 model), a larger windshield, and a sweeping new wraparound window at the tailgate. The Nomad, model #1793/6-cylinder, cost $2,728 and model #1893 with a V-8, the more popular of the two versions, cost $2,835, making it the most expensive Chevrolet in 1958 (with the exception of the Corvette).

Because the Nomad was now part of the Bel Air line, there were other exterior features that set this series apart from the Brookwood and Yeoman wagons. The front fenders were embossed with four distinctive stripes, as were the rear fenders. The script nameplate appeared on the rear fender.

The Nomad still carried the stainless ribbed bars on the tailgate. In 1958, station wagons had a single taillight instead of the three on the passenger cars.

In 1958, Chevrolet's new topgate design provided new floor to ceiling loading height. And the new link-type tailgate supports let the tailgate fold down level with the interior flooring.

The 1958 Brookwood station wagon was available either as a 6-passenger model #1593/6-cylinder or 9-passenger model #1693/8-cylinder. The 9-passenger wagons were models #1594/6-cylinder and #1694/8-cylinder. The 6-passenger cars sold for $2,574, and the 9-passenger vehicles for $2,785. Beginning in 1958, sales totals were released by body type, not by series. Thus, there were 187,063 wagons sold in 1958 (16,590 2-door models and 170,473 4-door models). The 9-passenger version had three seats. Lift out the third seat, fold down the second seat, and you had almost 88 cubic feet of space.

The budget wagon for 1958 was the Yeoman, available in 2- or 4-door versions. The interior featured vinyl upholstery, rubber floor mats, and linoleum rear floor covering, making the interior completely washable. This was an ideal car for gardeners, sportsmen, or a family with several young children.

Yeoman model numbers were: 2-door (#1191/6-cylinder and #1291/V-8) and 4-door (#1193/6-cylinder and #1293/V-8). The wagons cost respectively: $2,413, $2,520, $2,467 and $2,574. Two-tone cars were still popular, and Chevrolet offered 14 different ones to choose from. New colors this year included Silver Blue, Anniversary Gold (to celebrate GM's 50th anniversary in 1958), Aegean Turquoise, Cashmere Blue, Glen Green, and Honey Beige.

"All new all over again!" was how Chevrolet introduced the 1959 models in October 1958. Again this year the Nomad was the most luxurious wagon. There were two wagons, the Kingswood and Parkwood, that carried Bel Air trim, and the lower-priced Brookwood to round out the fleet for 1959. The most obvious styling changes for 1959 were the rear horizontal fins and cat's eye taillights. According to Tom McCahill, "Chevrolet will go down as the 1959 car with the wildest styling, barring none." Other noticeable changes from 1958 to 1959 include modifications in the grille, headlights, and parking lights, and a larger wraparound windshield.

The 1959 Nomad, model #1735/6-cylinder and #1835/V-8, was a 4-door, 6-passenger wagon and carried the Impala exterior trim. New this year was a retractable window that rolled down into the tailgate. Again, the Nomad was the most expensive model in the line-up selling for $2,891 with a 6-cylinder and $3,009 for the V-8 optioned model.

The Kingswood was Chevrolet's only 9-passenger car for 1959. Available in 6-cylinder (model #1545) and V-8 version (model #1645), this wagon also featured a power-operated retractable rear window.

New for 1959 was the new Lookout Lounge third seat which enabled passengers to watch the scenery glide past. When not in use, the third seat folded down out of the way to make room for cargo. Like the Nomad, the Kingswood interior was a combination of leathergrained vinyl and pattern cloth upholstery.

77

In 1958, the second mid-range station wagon, the Parkwood was available only as a 4-door, 6-passenger vehicle. Again, depending on the engine, there were two model numbers, #1535 with 6-cylinders and #1635 with the V-8. There were five leather-grained vinyl and pattern cloth upholstery combinations from which to select. The second seat folded down to provide for increased luggage/cargo space.

Sales materials described the 1959 Brookwood station wagon as having "Chevy beauty, Chevy economy, Chevy performance and Chevy utility at a price within the reach of any wagon owner." Available in both 2- and 4-door versions, with an all-vinyl interior, the Brookwood models #1115, #1135, #1215, and #1235 cost respectively $2,571, $2,638, $2,689 and $2,756 depending on the engine selected (6-cylinder or V-8).

Production for 2-door station wagons in 1959 was 20,760 and 188,623 for 4-door wagons. Unfortunately the all-new Chevrolets for 1959 did not meet with expectations and for the third time in six years Ford and Chevrolet were in a neck-in-neck race. There was also a sense that perhaps the design went a little too far. Most felt that it was time to return to a more conventional design. This is a 1959 Brookwood, 2-door, 6-passenger wagon, model #1215.

The 1960 Nomad, model #1735 (with 6-cylinder) and #1835 (with V-8), was a 4-door, 6-passenger wagon. Distinguishing characteristics include the two pairs of bar moldings above and below the molding strip on the front fenders, and the quarter panel missile-inspired ornaments with a white insert and Nomad nameplate set within.

Another view of Chevrolet's most expensive model, the 1960 Nomad. Nomads with 6-cylinder engines cost $2,889 and with a V-8, $2,996. Some popular colors for 1960 included Sateen Silver, Cascade Green, Tasco Turquoise, Fawn Beige, Suntan Copper, Shadow Gray, and Jade Green. There were 12 two-tone paint options to enhance the grace and dignity of Chevrolet's new appearance.

Again for 1960, the Kingwood was the only 9-passenger wagon. Like other wagons, it too was available as a 6-cylinder model #1545 and a V-8 version, model #1645. The Kingswood cost $2,850 (6-cylinder) and $2,957 (V-8). Station wagon production for 1960 was 14,663 (2-door units) and 198,066 (4-door units) for a total of 212,729 wagons.

In 1960, the missile-inspired side trim is present along with the new oval grille that enclosed dual headlights. Missing is the stainless strip that ran the length of the car in 1959.

The Brookwood station wagon was available as a 2-door model, #1115 (6-cylinder) and #1215 (V-8), and 4-door, #1135 (6-cylinder) and #1235 (V-8); the wagons cost $2,586, $2,693, $2,653 and $2,760 respectively.

Marketed as "The Greatest Show on Worth" with "parkable size," the new 1961 Chevrolets offered redesigned full-size cars again. This year there were ten station wagons, including four new Corvair wagons. Indeed owners of the 1961 Chevrolets found a "trim new size... clean new style... [and] fine new comfort." In 1961 there was a 9-passenger model in each station wagon series (Nomad, Parkwood and Brookwood).

The 1961 Nomad was available as a 6- or 9-passenger car with 6-cylinder or V-8. Deluxe wheel discs and wide side-moldings; contrasting insert panels were distinctive features of the Nomad. Crossed racing flags and the Nomad nameplate appeared within the insert panel on the rear fender. There were 24 power teams from which to select in 1961. The HI-THRIFT 6 was the industry's most refined 6-cylinder engine. V-8 choices included the ECONOMY TURBO-FIRE, SUPER TURBO-FIRE, TURBO-THRUST, and SUPER TURBO-THRUST. There were also five transmissions including the 3-speed synchromesh, overdrive, 4-speed synchromesh, Powerglide and Turboglide.

Standard Nomad luxury features included electric clock, parking brake warning light, back-up lights, deluxe window cranks, fingertip door releases, and extra-long armrests with built-in safety reflectors. The interior of durable new fabrics was available in six color combinations. Based on the engine selected, the cost of the Nomad began at $2,899 and went to $3,099, still the most expensive car in the Chevrolet line-up for 1961 (not counting the Corvette).

A chrome trim bar, extending from the front fender rearward, distinguished the 1961 Parkwood from the Brookwood station wagons. Parkwood nameplates appeared on the upper rear fender. The Parkwood was available like other wagons in both 6- and 9-passenger models. All 1961 station wagons were 4-door models. Prices for the Parkwood ranged from $2,747 to $2,957.

The 1961 Brookwood, like the Nomad and Parkwood, was available as a 6- or 9-passenger vehicle and included the following standard features: foam cushioned front seat, dual sun visors, two armrests, and glove box lock. Trim and upholstery were available in three color choices, and the rubber vinyl-coated floor mats blended with the interior colors. There was a new hidden stowage space concealed under the rear floor providing a compartment for valuables. Each wagon also featured bumper steps making it easier for passengers to climb into the third seat of the 9-passenger wagons. Station wagon production for 1961 breaks down accordingly: 31,649 three-seat units and 137,300 two-seat units for a total production of 168,949.

The Corvair, introduced originally in 1960, was expanded in 1961 to include two station wagons and the Greenbrier Sports Wagon, also available in two different models. There was a unique combination of economy and performance available in engines and transmissions for the 1961 Corvair. You could select from the Turbo-Air 6 80-horsepower or Super Turbo-Air 6 98-horsepower, in combination with one of three transmissions (3-speed synchromesh, Powerglide, or 4-speed synchromesh). The Lakewood 700 station wagon, model #0735, and the Lakewood 500 station wagon, model #0535, were both rear engine design vehicles that offered conventional station wagon space plus a separate, key-locking front trunk space of 10 cubic feet, providing a total cargo space of 68 cubic feet. There was full 6-passenger seating with the second seat up and when the seat was down, there was a cargo deck that extended to almost 6 1/2 feet long.

LAKEWOOD 500 4-DOOR STATION WAGON in Tuxedo Black. Lowest priced Corvair Station Wagon offers front and rear carrying space, totaling 68 cu. ft.

LAKEWOOD 700 4-DOOR STATION WAGON in Seafoam Green. Note the rear canopy shape, the perfect design for fresh outside styling.

Both 1961 Lakewood station wagons featured smart, durable easy-to-care-for interiors. There was a fabric-vinyl combination in four-color blends keyed to the exterior in the 700 series and an all-vinyl interior in three two-tone blends matching the exterior of the 500s. A simple motion opened the one-piece, counterbalanced liftgate. There were 5,591 Lakewood 500 wagons produced, each selling at a cost of $2,266 and 20,451 Lakewood 700s at a cost of $2,330 each.

The 1961 Corvair Greenbrier Sports Wagon was the "most versatile wagon in the world" according to Chevrolet marketing. Offered in two models—Greenbrier and Greenbrier DeLuxe—there was almost 175.5 cubic feet of cargo space, close to twice what you find in a regular station wagon. Standard features on the Greenbrier Sports Wagon included bright metal bumpers, hubcaps, four color-keyed interiors including spare tire cover and vinyl-coated floor mats, front armrests, foam-cushioned seats and seat backs. Roof rack, window screens, and interior tables were available at extra cost. Model year production reached 18,487 at a cost of $2,651 each.

In 1962, Chevrolet added the Chevy II line. Designed to compete with Ford's Falcon, the Chevy II, Chevrolet's thrift car, was available originally in four different series—100, 200, 300, and 400. The 200 series was discontinued shortly after introduction. This Chevy II 400 Nova station wagon, model #0435, cost $2,497 new. It came with a 6-cylinder engine, rear fender nameplates, side body, window and deck trim, rocker sill strips, front fender tip windsplit moldings, and full wheel discs. Deluxe heater and defroster, front and rear armrests, rear ash trays, dual sun visors, and cigarette lighter were standard features on the Nova 400.

The 1962 Chevy II 300 series was available with either a 4-cylinder (model #0345) or 6-cylinder (model #2855) engine. Both were 9-passenger cars. The 300 series lacked the rocker panel sills and deluxe wheel covers. A power-operated rear window was standard on the 300 series (optional on the 400 and 100 series). The 300 series sold for $2,517 and $2,577 based on the engine selected.

The interior of a 1962 Chevy II wagon. The second and rear-facing third seats fold down to provide over nine feet of cargo space with a total load capacity of 76.2 cubic feet.

This photo is dated December 20, 1960 and apparently identifies the yet unnamed Chevy II as model "XP-726." Other details accompanying the photograph suggest that this model was fiberglass.

The 1962 Chevy II 100 series station wagon, model #0135 (4-cylinder) and model #0235 (6-cylinder). The 100 series sold for $2,339 and $2,399 respectively. Popular colors for the Chevy II were Twilight Turquoise, Nassau Blue, Satin Silver, Roman Red, Adobe Beige, and Autumn Gold.

There were two Corvair station wagons for 1962. The 700 series, model #0735, and the new top-of-the-line Monza, model #0935. Neither wagon saw large production numbers—3,716 for the 700 series and 2,362 for the Monza, making the Monza the rarest of Corvairs for 1962. The 700 series cost $2,407 and the Monza, $2,569.

In 1962 the full-size cars were once again restyled. A lattice-type grille of anodized aluminum, dual headlights and parking/direction signals recessed in the grille, sculptured lines running along the front of the hood and along the fenders, impressive front bumpers, and a compound-curved windshield are a few of the distinguishing features for the model year. This is the 1962 Impala station wagon, model #1845. New, it cost $3,171.

There was a new family of station wagons for 1962: 6- and 9-passenger versions of the Impala and Bel Air, and the 6-passenger Biscayne (lowest priced of all the Chevrolet wagons). There were 6-cylinder and V-8 versions of each wagon series. Prices ranged from $2,725 (Biscayne, model #1135) to $3,171 (Impala, model #1845). This is the Bel Air, model #1645. In 1962 this model cost $3,029 with a V-8.

The 1962 Biscayne 6-passenger station wagon, model #1235.

Again in 1962 Corvair offered the Greenbrier Sports Wagon and the DeLuxe version of the same wagon. There was almost 175.5 cubic feet of space—nearly twice as much as can be found in regular station wagons.

In 1963 Chevrolet offered its widest range of models. There were five full-size station wagon models in three series with 6- or 9-passenger seating, and three Chevy II wagons: the 6-passenger Nova 400 and Chevy II 100, and the 3-seat Chevy II 300 9-passenger. There was a new standard 6, an improved V-8, and a brand new optional 409 V-8. Altogether, you could choose from seven different engines, each equipped with new battery-saving Delcotron generators, and four transmissions. There were new self-adjusting safety-master brakes, extended life exhaust, and new air-washed rocker panels to combat the problem of rocker rust and corrosion. Each model received a facelift with an emphasis on making Chevrolets look more like luxury cars. The use of brightwork and changing the bodyside contours made the changes from 1962 to 1963 appear greater than they actually were.

The 1963 Chevrolet Impala station wagon, models #1735, #1745, #1835, and #1845 (depending on engine selected) offered an upholstered interior in smooth fabric and vinyl, or all vinyl. Standard features included deep-twist carpeting, electric clock, parking brake warning light, back-up lights, and fingertip door releases. A hidden compartment beneath the rear cargo floor provided 10.5 cubic feet of storage space.

Marketing materials suggested that the 1963 Impala station wagon "sets an elegant trend in full-size wagons." Impala wagons ranged in price from a low of $2,960 (6-cylinder version) to a high of $3,170 (9-passenger, V-8 version).

Again, in 1963 there really wasn't much difference between the Bel Air and Biscayne models. A bright metal lower body ridge molding on the Bel Air was absent on the Biscayne. Marketing suggested that the Bel Air was a "family wagon favorite built for enjoyment," while the Biscayne was "the easiest to buy of all new full-size Chevrolet wagons." Bel Air models ranged in price from $2,818 to $3,028 and the Biscayne wagons $2,723 to $2,830. There were 198,542 full-size wagons produced in 1963.

This 1963 Chevrolet Chevy II Nova 400 station wagon is a "Super Sport" model. When ordered with this optional package the car was trimmed out with special finned wheel covers, wider bodyside trim moldings, aluminized rear panels, and "SS" badges on the rear fenders and right-hand side of the deck lid.

CHEVY II 300

Chevy II 300 4-Door 3-Seat Station Wagon in Monaco B[...]

"Fashioned with a flair for family fun..." the 1963 Chevy II 300 station wagon (model #0345 or #0445, depending on the engine selected) was "family-priced for even the most modest budget." Standard luxuries included power-operated tailgate window, twin sun visors, foam-cushioned front seats, and automatic interior light switches.

"The perfect way to stretch your wagon dollars without sacrificing beauty and practicality." The 1963 Chevy II 100 station wagon offered many of the same features as the 300 and 400 series. The all-vinyl interior made clean-up time a breeze. The Chevy II 100 series, model #0135 and #0235, cost $2,338 and $2,397 respectively. There were 75,274 Chevy II wagons produced in 1963.

CHEVY II 100

Chevy II 100 4-Door 6-Passenger Station Wagon in Adobe Beige with Roof Luggage Carrier.

106

The 1963 Corvair Greenbrier Sports Wagon was the only station wagon in the Corvair line for 1963. Gone were the Monza and 500 series wagons. Intended for business and pleasure, the Greenbrier Sport Wagon could be fitted with a third seat, making it a 9-passenger wagon. A "Camping Gear" option was also available. Almost everything one needed to personalize the Greenbrier for outdoor activities was provided in this one package. The Greenbrier was offered in 1964 and then discontinued.

CORVAIR GREENBRIER SPORTS WAGON

Corvair Greenbrier De Luxe Sports Wagon in Cardinal Red and Cameo White

There were only minor style changes to the model line-up in 1964. Color-accented bodyside moldings, hood and deck windsplit moldings, rear cove outline moldings, and bright belt moldings are a few of the changes used to distinguish one model from another. The mid-size Chevelle was introduced and now there were 43 models in five different car lines. The Chevy II 300 series wagon was discontinued, but there were two new Chevelle wagons added. Dealer introduction of the new models occurred on September 28, 1963.

Described as the "wagon world's newcomer with winning ways," the 1964 Chevelle Malibu station wagon, available as a 6- or 9-passenger car with 6-cylinder or V-8 power, offered loads of family room, fashionably designed interiors, and all of Chevrolet's traditional value and reliability. The Chevelle Malibu wagon ranged in price from $2,647 (4-door, 6-passenger, 6-cylinder) to $2,852 (4-door, 9-passenger, V-8).

The 1964 Chevelle 300 station wagon was available as a 2- or 4-door model with 6 or 9 passenger space. There were four engine and four transmission choices to select from. The Chevelle 300 wagons had up to 86.0 cubic feet of usable cargo space. The upholstery was a durable pattern cloth with vinyl trim. The cost of this wagon ranged from $2,528 to $2,674. In total, there were 44,000 Chevelle wagons produced in 1964.

The 1964 Chevy II had a redesigned grille, no belt moldings on the 100 series, and a nameplate on the rear fender; the Nova had belt moldings from the front to the rear fender and a nameplate on the rear edge of the front fender. The vinyl interiors and deep-twist carpeting were attractive. The mono-plate rear springs gave Chevy II its smooth, steady control on the road. Two unitized box-like sections form the basic body assembly.

In 1964, there were still three different full-size wagon models—the Impala, the Bel Air, and the Biscayne. Each was available as a 6- or 9-passenger 4-door with seven engines and four transmissions from which to choose. The most expensive wagon, the Impala, model #1845, cost $3,181 and the least expensive, the Biscayne, model #1135, cost $2,763. There were 192,800 station wagons produced in 1964.

The appearance of the full-size Chevrolets changed dramatically in 1965. The bodies were larger, there was a new grille, the parking lights were just below the front bumper and centered between the dual headlights, and the rear-end styling featured triple taillight clusters (Impala) and bright rear cover panel trim. There was also chrome trim around each taillight and, depending on the model, full-length bodyside moldings and nameplate identification—front fender on Impala and rear quarter panels on Bel Air and Biscayne. The Impala station wagon was "as much at home with Sunday's best..." as it was "with Saturday's bushel baskets." In this wagon you could haul up to 106 cubic feet of goods. Available in both 6- and 9-passenger versions, the Impala offered woodgrained lower instrument panel facings and luxurious vinyl upholstery. Interestingly, there was no change in price in the Impala 9-passenger wagon from 1964 to 1965; there was, however, an increase of one dollar in the 6-passenger model.

The station wagon, a 1965 Impala in this case, with optional roof rack, was certainly no stranger to the suburban housewife in the mid-1960s. Chevrolet pursued a recreational theme during the late 1950s and this expanded into the 1960s with advertising reflecting the many uses of a station wagon in the daily routine of the family.

The 1965 Chevrolet Biscayne 4-door station wagon. A quick check and you can see that this model again lacks the bright trim and bodyside moldings shared by the Impala and Bel Air. There were 184,400 full-size wagons produced in 1965.

The 1965 Chevelle, the mid-size Chevrolet, also enjoyed a makeover. There was a new hood, grille, bumper, and front fenders. Curved side glass, refined front and rear suspension, added body insulation for a quieter, smoother ride, and 16 power teams to fit any kind of performance rounded out the changes for 1965. There were two Chevelle wagons again—the Chevelle Malibu and the Chevelle 300 DeLuxe wagon. The lack of bright bodyside trim strips and rear fender nameplates were two differences between the two models. Each was a 6-passenger, 4-door wagon. Total Chevelle output for 1965 was 37,600 units.

The 1965 Chevrolet Chevy IIs were mildly restyled with a new grille, new rear cove treatment, and new bodyside trim. The Nova featured full-length, color-accented bodyside moldings, and Nova nameplate and emblems on the rear fenders. There were 21,500 Chevy II station wagons built in 1965.

This was the second year of a total redesign and, thus, there were only minor changes in the 1966 Chevrolets. Chevelle and Chevy II models were restyled. The "427" V-8 was added to the engine line-up. And if you count the new Sportvan, available in three models, there were 14 models of wagons to choose from. Can you name the wagons in this photograph? From left to right: Chevrolet Caprice, Impala, Bel Air, Biscayne, Chevelle Malibu, and Chevy II Nova.

The Caprice was originally an option package in 1965, but in 1966 it became a series of its own. In the series were a Custom Coupe with unique roofline, and two station wagons. The Caprice Custom station wagons, model #16635 (4-door, 2-seat) and model #16645 (4-door, 3-seat), were distinguished from the other wagons in 1966 by woodgrained bodyside trim. All vinyl interiors were available in fawn, turquoise, red, blue, green, or black. The instrument cluster, trimmed with the look of hand-rubbed walnut and deep-twist carpet round out the attention to interior detail found on the Caprice Custom station wagons. The Caprice Custom 3-seat wagon (with rear-facing third seat) cost $3,347 and the 2-seat version, $3,234.

Advertising in 1966 wanted to demonstrate the versatility of the new 1966 Caprice Custom station wagon. In line with Chevrolet marketing there continued to be references to both family and recreation. Seems like everyone is ready but dad!

The 1966 Impala station wagon, available as 2- and 3-seat versions, garnered color-accented full-length bodyside molding, body sill moldings, bright trim around the windows, Impala nameplates on the front fender, deck lid moldings, and dual-unit wraparound taillights. There were seven engines to select from plus Chevrolet's newest automatic transmission, the Turbo Hydra-Matic. Another new comfort feature available was the tilt-telescopic steering wheel... isn't it amazing how much we take for granted today? The Impala station wagon, depending on whether a 6-cylinder or V-8 was selected, cost $2,971, $3,083, $3,076 and $3,189 respectively.

"Whether you're headed for the club in the chic 4-door, 2-seater, or headed for the park with the Cub Scout pack in the 3-seater (just as chic), you'll be right at home in the Bel Air."

Another view of an attractive Bel Air station wagon. This one features the optional luggage rack; an additional cost of $43. The Bel Air wagons cost $2,835, $2,940, $2,948 and $3,053 respectively, depending on seats and engines.

The 1966 Chevrolet Biscayne station wagon continued to provide "style conscious space at a modest price.... Or, another way to size it: 106.1 cubic feet of load space.... Cross country or across town, this wagon makes good traveling sense." Paying $2,772 put you into a Biscayne wagon. Full-size wagon production for 1966 was approximatcly 185,500.

The 1966 Chevelle series received new body contour lines, a wider grille, new rear body cove treatment, curved side glass, massive new bumpers, new tailgate ornamentation with full-width ribbed molding, and vertical taillights. There were two wagons, the Malibu and the 300 DeLuxe. Both were 4-door, 2-seat versions. The Chevelle wagon was "a versatile wagon that turns on the charm... [and] mixes great with young families and young budgets." There were 31,900 Chevelle wagons produced.

The 1966 Chevy II series offered an "exciting new wagon look in the lower price field," emphatically all new from the grille to the newly styled tailgate. Surprisingly well appointed and spacious, the interior was all vinyl with deep-twist carpeting. There were two models, the Chevy II Nova and the Chevy II 100. Priced at $2,430 and $2,518 respectively, there were 21,400 Chevy II wagons produced in 1966.

Added to the Chevrolet wagon line in 1966 was the Sportvan. Available in three models—the Deluxe Sportvan, the Custom Sportvan, and the Sportvan, all three "open[s] doors to wagon-going pleasure for work or play." You could specify either one or two removable rear seats. With both installed, eight passengers could ride comfortably. The seats could face either the front or the rear, or be removed. With the extra seats out there was a full 211.2 cubic feet of load space. The Sportvan came from the G-1200 series of Chevrolet van panel trucks.

MORE TITLES FROM ICONOGRAFIX:

AMERICAN CULTURE

AMERICAN SERVICE STATIONS 1935-1943 PHOTO ARCHIVE	ISBN 1-882256-27-1
COCA-COLA: A HISTORY IN PHOTOGRAPHS 1930-1969	ISBN 1-882256-46-8
COCA-COLA: ITS VEHICLES IN PHOTOGRAPHS 1930-1969	ISBN 1-882256-47-6
PHILLIPS 66 1945-1954 PHOTO ARCHIVE	ISBN 1-882256-42-5
RVs & CAMPERS 1900-2000: AN ILLUSTRATED HISTORY	ISBN 1-58388-064-X

AUTOMOTIVE

AMX PHOTO ARCHIVE: FROM CONCEPT TO REALITY	ISBN 1-58388-062-3
CADILLAC 1948-1964 PHOTO ALBUM	ISBN 1-882256-83-2
CAMARO 1967-2000 PHOTO ARCHIVE	ISBN 1-58388-032-1
CHEVROLET STATION WAGONS 1946-1966 PHOTO ARCHIVE	ISBN 1-58388-069-0
CLASSIC AMERICAN LIMOUSINES 1955-2000 PHOTO ARCHIVE	ISBN 1-58388-041-0
CORVAIR by CHEVROLET EXP. & PROD. CARS 1957-1969 LUDVIGSEN LIBRARY SERIES	ISBN 1-58388-058-5
CORVETTE THE EXOTIC EXPERIMENTAL CARS, LUDVIGSEN LIBRARY SERIES	ISBN 1-58388-017-8
CORVETTE PROTOTYPES & SHOW CARS PHOTO ALBUM	ISBN 1-882256-77-8
EARLY FORD V-8S 1932-1942 PHOTO ALBUM	ISBN 1-882256-97-2
IMPERIAL 1955-1963 PHOTO ARCHIVE	ISBN 1-882256-22-0
IMPERIAL 1964-1968 PHOTO ARCHIVE	ISBN 1-882256-23-9
LINCOLN MOTOR CARS 1920-1942 PHOTO ARCHIVE	ISBN 1-882256-57-3
LINCOLN MOTOR CARS 1946-1960 PHOTO ARCHIVE	ISBN 1-882256-58-1
PACKARD MOTOR CARS 1935-1942 PHOTO ARCHIVE	ISBN 1-882256-44-1
PACKARD MOTOR CARS 1946-1958 PHOTO ARCHIVE	ISBN 1-882256-45-X
PONTIAC DREAM CARS, SHOW CARS & PROTOTYPES 1928-1998 PHOTO ALBUM	ISBN 1-882256-93-X
PONTIAC FIREBIRD TRANS-AM 1969-1999 PHOTO ALBUM	ISBN 1-882256-95-6
PONTIAC FIREBIRD 1967-2000 PHOTO HISTORY	ISBN 1-58388-028-3
STRETCH LIMOUSINES 1928-2001 PHOTO ARCHIVE	ISBN 1-58388-070-4
STUDEBAKER 1933-1942 PHOTO ARCHIVE	ISBN 1-882256-24-7
ULTIMATE CORVETTE TRIVIA CHALLENGE	ISBN 1-58388-035-6

BUSES

BUSES OF MOTOR COACH INDUSTRIES 1932-2000 PHOTO ARCHIVE	ISBN 1-58388-039-9
FLXIBLE TRANSIT BUSES 1953-1995 PHOTO ARCHIVE	ISBN 1-58388-053-4
GREYHOUND BUSES 1914-2000 PHOTO ARCHIVE	ISBN 1-58388-027-5
MACK® BUSES 1900-1960 PHOTO ARCHIVE*	ISBN 1-58388-020-8
TRAILWAYS BUSES 1936-2001 PHOTO ARCHIVE	ISBN 1-58388-029-1
TROLLEY BUSES 1913-2001 PHOTO ARCHIVE	ISBN 1-58388-057-7
YELLOW COACH BUSES 1923-1943 PHOTO ARCHIVE	ISBN 1-58388-054-2

EMERGENCY VEHICLES

AMERICAN LAFRANCE 700 SERIES 1945-1952 PHOTO ARCHIVE	ISBN 1-882256-90-5
AMERICAN LAFRANCE 700 SERIES 1945-1952 PHOTO ARCHIVE VOLUME 2	ISBN 1-58388-025-9
AMERICAN LAFRANCE 700 & 800 SERIES 1953-1958 PHOTO ARCHIVE	ISBN 1-882256-91-3
AMERICAN LAFRANCE 900 SERIES 1958-1964 PHOTO ARCHIVE	ISBN 1-58388-002-X
CROWN FIRECOACH 1951-1985 PHOTO ARCHIVE	ISBN 1-58388-047-X
CLASSIC AMERICAN AMBULANCES 1900-1979 PHOTO ARCHIVE	ISBN 1-882256-94-8
CLASSIC AMERICAN FUNERAL VEHICLES 1900-1980 PHOTO ARCHIVE	ISBN 1-58388-016-X
CLASSIC SEAGRAVE 1935-1951 PHOTO ARCHIVE	ISBN 1-58388-034-8
FIRE CHIEF CARS 1900-1997 PHOTO ALBUM	ISBN 1-882256-87-5
HEAVY RESCUE TRUCKS 1931-2000 PHOTO GALLERY	ISBN 1-58388-045-3
INDUSTRIAL AND PRIVATE FIRE APPARATUS 1925-2001 PHOTO ARCHIVE	ISBN 1-58388-049-6
LOS ANGELES CITY FIRE APPARATUS 1953 - 1999 PHOTO ARCHIVE	ISBN 1-58388-012-7
MACK MODEL C FIRE TRUCKS 1957-1967 PHOTO ARCHIVE*	ISBN 1-58388-014-3
MACK MODEL L FIRE TRUCKS 1940-1954 PHOTO ARCHIVE*	ISBN 1-882256-86-7
MAXIM FIRE APPARATUS 1914-1989 PHOTO ARCHIVE	ISBN 1-58388-050-X
NAVY & MARINE CORPS FIRE APPARATUS 1836 -2000 PHOTO GALLERY	ISBN 1-58388-031-3
POLICE CARS: RESTORING, COLLECTING & SHOWING AMERICA'S FINEST SEDANS	ISBN 1-58388-046-1
SEAGRAVE 70TH ANNIVERSARY SERIES PHOTO ARCHIVE	ISBN 1-58388-001-1
TASC FIRE APPARATUS 1946-1985 PHOTO ARCHIVE	ISBN 1-58388-065-8
VOLUNTEER & RURAL FIRE APPARATUS PHOTO GALLERY	ISBN 1-58388-005-4
W.S. DARLEY & CO. FIRE APPARATUS 1908-2000 PHOTO ACHIVE	ISBN 1-58388-061-5
WARD LAFRANCE FIRE TRUCKS 1918-1978 PHOTO ARCHIVE	ISBN 1-58388-013-5
WILDLAND FIRE APPARATUS 1940-2001 PHOTO GALLERY	ISBN 1-58388-056-9
YOUNG FIRE EQUIPMENT 1932-1991 PHOTO ARCHIVE	ISBN 1-58388-015-1

RACING

CHAPARRAL CAN-AM RACING CARS FROM TEXAS LUDVIGSEN LIBRARY SERIES	ISBN 1-58388-066-6
DRAG RACING FUNNY CARS OF THE 1970s PHOTO ARCHIVE	ISBN 1-58388-068-2
EL MIRAGE IMPRESSIONS: DRY LAKES LAND SPEED RACING	ISBN 1-58388-059-3
GT40 PHOTO ARCHIVE	ISBN 1-882256-64-6
INDY CARS OF THE 1950s, LUDVIGSEN LIBRARY SERIES	ISBN 1-58388-018-6
INDY CARS OF THE 1960s, LUDVIGSEN LIBRARY SERIES	ISBN 1-58388-052-6
INDIANAPOLIS RACING CARS OF FRANK KURTIS 1941-1963 PHOTO ARCHIVE	ISBN 1-58388-026-7
JUAN MANUEL FANGIO WORLD CHAMPION DRIVER SERIES PHOTO ALBUM	ISBN 1-58388-008-9
LE MANS 1950 PHOTO ARCHIVE THE BRIGGS CUNNINGHAM CAMPAIGN	ISBN 1-882256-21-2
MARIO ANDRETTI WORLD CHAMPION DRIVER SERIES PHOTO ALBUM	ISBN 1-58388-009-7
MERCEDES-BENZ 300SL RACING CARS 1952-1953 LUDVIGSEN LIBRARY SERIES	ISBN 1-58388-067-4
NOVI V-8 INDY CARS 1941-1965 LUDVIGSEN LIBRARY SERIES	ISBN 1-58388-037-2
SEBRING 12-HOUR RACE 1970 PHOTO ARCHIVE	ISBN 1-882256-20-4
VANDERBILT CUP RACE 1936 & 1937 PHOTO ARCHIVE	ISBN 1-882256-66-2

RAILWAYS

CHICAGO, ST. PAUL, MINNEAPOLIS & OMAHA RAILWAY 1880-1940 PHOTO ARCHIVE	ISBN 1-882256-67-0
CHICAGO & NORTH WESTERN RAILWAY 1975-1995 PHOTO ARCHIVE	ISBN 1-882256-76-X
GREAT NORTHERN RAILWAY 1945-1970 PHOTO ARCHIVE	ISBN 1-882256-56-5
GREAT NORTHERN RAILWAY 1945-1970 VOL 2 PHOTO ARCHIVE	ISBN 1-882256-79-4
ILLINOIS CENTRAL RAILROAD 1854-1960 PHOTO ARCHIVE	ISBN 1-58388-063-1
MILWAUKEE ROAD 1850-1960 PHOTO ARCHIVE	ISBN 1-882256-61-1
MILWAUKEE ROAD DEPOTS 1856-1954 PHOTO ARCHIVE	ISBN 1-58388-040-2
SHOW TRAINS OF THE 20TH CENTURY	ISBN 1-58388-030-5
SOO LINE 1975-1992 PHOTO ARCHIVE	ISBN 1-882256-68-9
TRAINS OF THE TWIN PORTS, DULUTH-SUPERIOR IN THE 1950s PHOTO ARCHIVE	ISBN 1-58388-003-8
TRAINS OF THE CIRCUS 1872-1956	ISBN 1-58388-024-0
TRAINS of the UPPER MIDWEST PHOTO ARCHIVE STEAM&DIESEL in the1950S&1960S	ISBN 1-58388-036-4
WISCONSIN CENTRAL LIMITED 1987-1996 PHOTO ARCHIVE	ISBN 1-882256-75-1
WISCONSIN CENTRAL RAILWAY 1871-1909 PHOTO ARCHIVE	ISBN 1-882256-78-6

TRUCKS

BEVERAGE TRUCKS 1910-1975 PHOTO ARCHIVE	ISBN 1-882256-60-3
BROCKWAY TRUCKS 1948-1961 PHOTO ARCHIVE*	ISBN 1-882256-55-7
CHEVROLET EL CAMINO PHOTO HISTORY INCL GMC SPRINT & CABALLERO	ISBN 1-58388-044-5
CIRCUS AND CARNIVAL TRUCKS 1923-2000 PHOTO ARCHIVE	ISBN 1-58388-048-8
DODGE PICKUPS 1939-1978 PHOTO ALBUM	ISBN 1-882256-82-4
DODGE POWER WAGONS 1940-1980 PHOTO ARCHIVE	ISBN 1-882256-89-1
DODGE POWER WAGON PHOTO HISTORY	ISBN 1-58388-019-4
DODGE RAM TRUCKS 1994-2001 PHOTO HISTORY	ISBN 1-58388-051-8
DODGE TRUCKS 1929-1947 PHOTO ARCHIVE	ISBN 1-882256-36-0
DODGE TRUCKS 1948-1960 PHOTO ARCHIVE	ISBN 1-882256-37-9
FORD HEAVY-DUTY TRUCKS 1948-1998 PHOTO HISTORY	ISBN 1-58388-043-7
JEEP 1941-2000 PHOTO ARCHIVE	ISBN 1-58388-021-6
JEEP PROTOTYPES & CONCEPT VEHICLES PHOTO ARCHIVE	ISBN 1-58388-033-X
LOGGING TRUCKS 1915-1970 PHOTO ARCHIVE	ISBN 1-882256-59-X
MACK MODEL AB PHOTO ARCHIVE*	ISBN 1-882256-18-2
MACK AP SUPER-DUTY TRUCKS 1926-1938 PHOTO ARCHIVE*	ISBN 1-882256-54-9
MACK MODEL B 1953-1966 VOL 1 PHOTO ARCHIVE*	ISBN 1-882256-19-0
MACK MODEL B 1953-1966 VOL 2 PHOTO ARCHIVE*	ISBN 1-882256-34-4
MACK EB-EC-ED-EE-EF-EG-DE 1936-1951 PHOTO ARCHIVE*	ISBN 1-882256-29-8
MACK EH-EJ-EM-EQ-ER-ES 1936-1950 PHOTO ARCHIVE*	ISBN 1-882256-39-5
MACK FC-FCSW-NW 1936-1947 PHOTO ARCHIVE*	ISBN 1-882256-28-X
MACK FG-FH-FJ-FK-FN-FP-FT-FW 1937-1950 PHOTO ARCHIVE*	ISBN 1-882256-35-2
MACK LF-LH-LJ-LM-LT 1940-1956 PHOTO ARCHIVE*	ISBN 1-882256-38-7
MACK TRUCKS PHOTO GALLERY*	ISBN 1-882256-88-3
NEW CAR CARRIERS 1910-1998 PHOTO ALBUM	ISBN 1-882256-98-0
PLYMOUTH COMMERCIAL VEHICLES PHOTO ARCHIVE	ISBN 1-58388-004-6
REFUSE TRUCKS PHOTO ARCHIVE	ISBN 1-58388-042-9
STUDEBAKER TRUCKS 1927-1940 PHOTO ARCHIVE	ISBN 1-882256-40-9
STUDEBAKER TRUCKS 1941-1964 PHOTO ARCHIVE	ISBN 1-882256-41-7
WHITE TRUCKS 1900-1937 PHOTO ARCHIVE	ISBN 1-882256-80-8

TRACTORS & CONSTRUCTION EQUIPMENT

CASE TRACTORS 1912-1959 PHOTO ARCHIVE	ISBN 1-882256-32-8
CATERPILLAR PHOTO GALLERY	ISBN 1-882256-70-0
CATERPILLAR POCKET GUIDE THE TRACK-TYPE TRACTORS 1925-1957	ISBN 1-58388-022-4
CATERPILLAR D-2 & R-2 PHOTO ARCHIVE	ISBN 1-882256-99-9
CATERPILLAR D-8 1933-1974 PHOTO ARCHIVE INCLUDING DIESEL 75 & RD-8	ISBN 1-882256-96-4
CATERPILLAR MILITARY TRACTORS VOLUME 1 PHOTO ARCHIVE	ISBN 1-882256-16-6
CATERPILLAR MILITARY TRACTORS VOLUME 2 PHOTO ARCHIVE	ISBN 1-882256-17-4
CATERPILLAR SIXTY PHOTO ARCHIVE	ISBN 1-882256-05-0
CATERPILLAR TEN PHOTO ARCHIVE INCLUDING 7C FIFTEEN & HIGH FIFTEEN	ISBN 1-58388-011-9
CATERPILLAR THIRTY PHOTO ARCHIVE 2ND ED. INC. BEST THIRTY, 6G THIRTY & R-4	ISBN 1-58388-006-2
CLETRAC AND OLIVER CRAWLERS PHOTO ARCHIVE	ISBN 1-882256-43-3
CLASSIC AMERICAN STEAMROLLERS 1871-1935 PHOTO ARCHIVE	ISBN 1-58388-038-0
FARMALL CUB PHOTO ARCHIVE	ISBN 1-882256-71-9
FARMALL F- SERIES PHOTO ARCHIVE	ISBN 1-882256-02-6
FARMALL MODEL H PHOTO ARCHIVE	ISBN 1-882256-03-4
FARMALL MODEL M PHOTO ARCHIVE	ISBN 1-882256-15-8
FARMALL REGULAR PHOTO ARCHIVE	ISBN 1-882256-14-X
FARMALL SUPER SERIES PHOTO ARCHIVE	ISBN 1-882256-49-2
FORDSON 1917-1928 PHOTO ARCHIVE	ISBN 1-882256-33-6
HART-PARR PHOTO ARCHIVE	ISBN 1-882256-08-5
HOLT TRACTORS PHOTO ARCHIVE	ISBN 1-882256-10-7
INTERNATIONAL TRACTRACTOR PHOTO ARCHIVE	ISBN 1-882256-48-4
INTERNATIONAL TD CRAWLERS 1933-1962 PHOTO ARCHIVE	ISBN 1-882256-72-7
JOHN DEERE MODEL A PHOTO ARCHIVE	ISBN 1-882256-12-3
JOHN DEERE MODEL B PHOTO ARCHIVE	ISBN 1-882256-01-8
JOHN DEERE MODEL D PHOTO ARCHIVE	ISBN 1-882256-00-X
JOHN DEERE 30 SERIES PHOTO ARCHIVE	ISBN 1-882256-13-1
MARION CONSTRUCTION MACHINERY 1884 - 1975 PHOTO ARCHIVE	ISBN 1-58388-060-7
MINNEAPOLIS-MOLINE U-SERIES PHOTO ARCHIVE	ISBN 1-882256-07-7
OLIVER TRACTORS PHOTO ARCHIVE	ISBN 1-882256-09-3
RUSSELL GRADERS PHOTO ARCHIVE	ISBN 1-882256-11-5
TWIN CITY TRACTOR PHOTO ARCHIVE	ISBN 1-882256-06-9

*This product is sold under license from Mack Trucks, Inc. Mack is a registered Trademark of Mack Trucks, Inc. All rights reserved.

All Iconografix books are available from direct mail specialty book dealers and bookstores worldwide, or can be ordered from the publisher. For book trade and distribution information or to add your name to our mailing list and receive a **FREE CATALOG** contact:

Iconografix, PO Box 446, Hudson, Wisconsin, 54016 Telephone: (715) 381-9755, (800) 289-3504 (USA), Fax: (715) 381-9756

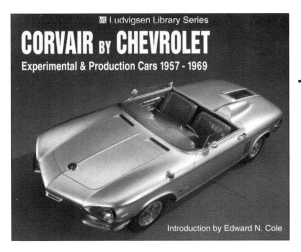
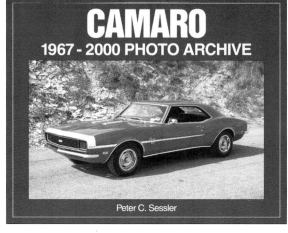

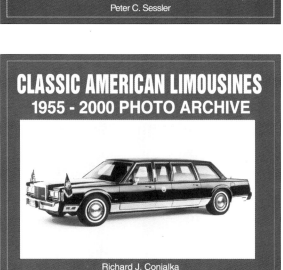
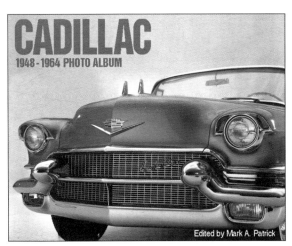
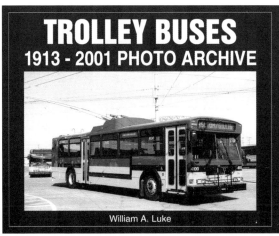
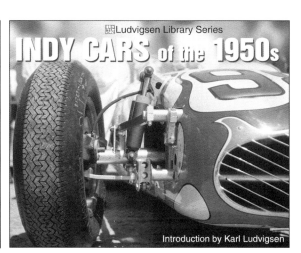